A Time t

A Time to Sing

100 hymns and songs for school worship

edited by

HAROLD CLARKE AND PETER KNEALE

MACMILLAN

First published 1984
Reprinted 1986, 1987, 1988, 1989, 1990

Published by
MACMILLAN EDUCATION LTD
Houndmills, Basingstoke, Hampshire RG21 2XS
and London
Companies and representatives
throughout the world

Printed in Hong Kong

ISBN 0–333–35991–7

CONTENTS

4: Our Daily Life

5: Lord Jesus Christ

6: Festival and Celebration

7: The Christmas Season

ALPHABETICAL INDEX OF FIRST LINES

1
GOD'S CREATION

1 All creatures of our God and King

1
All creatures of our God and King,
Lift up your voice and with us sing:
Alleluya, Alleluya!
Thou burning sun with golden beam,
Thou silver moon with softer gleam:

Chorus
O praise him, O praise him,
Alleluya, Alleluya, Alleluya!

2
Thou rushing wind that art so strong,
Ye clouds that sail in heaven along,
O praise him, Alleluya!
Thou rising morn, in praise rejoice,
Ye lights of evening, find a voice:

Chorus

3
Thou flowing water, pure and clear,
Make music for thy Lord to hear,
Alleluya, Alleluya!
Thou fire so masterful and bright,
That givest man both warmth and light:

Chorus

4
Let all things their creator bless,
And worship him in humbleness,
O praise him, Alleluya!
Praise, praise the Father, praise the Son,
And praise the Spirit, three in One:

Chorus

W H DRAPER BASED ON ST FRANCIS

2 All things bright and beautiful

Chorus
All things bright and beautiful,
All creatures great and small,
All things wise and wonderful,
The Lord God made them all.

1
Each little flower that opens,
Each little bird that sings,
He made their glowing colours,
He made their tiny wings:

Chorus

2
The purple-headed mountain,
The river running by,
The sunset and the morning
That brightens up the sky:

Chorus

3
The cold wind in the winter,
The pleasant summer sun,
The ripe fruits in the garden,—
He made them every one:

Chorus

4
He gave us eyes to see them,
And lips that we might tell
How great is God Almighty,
Who has made all things well:

Chorus

MRS C F ALEXANDER

3 All things which live below the sky

1
All things which live below the sky
Or move beneath the sea,
Are creatures of the Lord most high
And brothers unto me.

2
I love to hear the robin sing,
Perched on the highest bough;
To see the rook with purple wing
Follow the shining plough.

3
I love to watch the swallow skim
The river in his flight;
To mark, when day is growing dim,
The glow-worm's silvery light.

4
The seagull whiter than the foam,
The fish that dart beneath;
The lowing cattle coming home;
The goats upon the heath.

5
Almighty Father, King of Kings,
The lover of the meek,
Make me a friend of helpless things,
Defender of the weak.

E J BRAILSFORD

4 For the beauty of the earth

1
For the beauty of the earth,
For the beauty of the skies,
For the love which from our birth
Over and around us lies:

Chorus
Father, unto thee we raise,
This our sacrifice of praise.

2
For the beauty of each hour,
Of the day and of the night,
Hill and vale, and tree and flower,
Sun and moon and stars of light:

Chorus

3
For the joy of human love,
Brother, sister, parent, child.
Friends on earth, and friends above,
For all gentle thoughts and mild:

Chorus

4
For each perfect gift of thine
To our race so freely given,
Graces human and divine,
Flowers of earth and buds of heaven:

Chorus

FOLLIOTT SANDFORD PIERPOINT

5 God bless the grass

1
God bless the grass that grows through the crack,
They roll the concrete over it to try and keep it back.
The concrete gets tired of what it has to do,
It breaks and it buckles and the grass grows through;
And God bless the grass.

2
God bless the truth that fights toward the sun,
They roll the lies over it and hope that it is done.
It moves through the ground and reaches for the air,
And after a while it is growing everywhere;
And God bless the truth.

3
God bless the grass that breaks through cement.
It's green and it's tender and it's easily bent,
But after a while it lifts up its head,
For the grass is living and the stone is dead;
And God bless the grass.

4
God bless the grass that's gentle and low,
Its roots they are deep and its will is to grow.
And God bless the truth, the friend of the poor,
And the wild grass growing at the poor man's door;
And God bless the grass.

MALVINA REYNOLDS

6 He made me

1
He gave me eyes so I could see
The wonders of the world;
Without my eyes I could not see
The other boys and girls.
He gave me ears so I could hear
The wind and rain and sea.
I've got to tell it to the world,
He made me.

2
He gave me lips so I could speak
And say what's in my mind;
Without my lips I could not speak
A single word or line.
He made my mind so I could think,
And choose what I should be.
I've got to tell it to the world,
He made me.

3
He gave me hands so I could touch,
And hold a thousand things;
I need my hands to help me write,
To help me fetch and bring.
These feet he made so I could run,
He meant me to be free.
I've got to tell it to the world,
He made me.

ALAN PINNOCK

7 Morning has broken

1
Morning has broken,
Like the first morning.
Blackbird has spoken
Like the first bird.
Praise for the singing!
Praise for the morning!
Praise for them, springing
Fresh from the word!

2
Sweet the rain's new fall
Sunlit from heaven,
Like the first dewfall
On the first grass.
Praise for the sweetness
Of the wet garden,
Sprung in completeness
Where his feet pass.

3
Mine is the sunlight!
Mine is the morning
Born of the one light
Eden saw play!
Praise with elation,
Praise every morning,
God's re-creation
Of the new day!

ELEANOR FARJEON

8 Stand up, clap hands

Chorus
Stand up, clap hands, shout thank you Lord,
Thank you for the world I'm in.
Stand up, clap hands, shout thank you Lord
For happiness and peace within.

1
I look around and the sun's in the sky,
I look around and then I think oh my!
The world is such a wonderful place,
And all because of the Good Lord's grace.

Chorus

2
I look around and the creatures I see,
I look around and it amazes me,
That ev'ry fox and bird and hare,
Must fit in a special place somewhere.

Chorus

3
I look around at all the joy I've had,
I look around and then it makes me glad
That I can offer thanks and praise
To him who guides me through my days.

Chorus

ROGER DYER

9 The butterfly song

1
If I were a butterfly,
I'd thank you, Lord, for giving me wings,
And if I were a robin in a tree,
I'd thank you, Lord, that I could sing,
And if I were a fish in the sea,
I'd wiggle my tail and I'd giggle with glee,
But I just thank you, Father, for making me 'me'.

Chorus
For you gave me a heart and you gave me a smile,
You gave me Jesus and you made me your child,
And I just thank you, Father, for making me 'me'.

2
If I were an elephant,
I'd thank you, Lord, by raising my trunk,
And if I were a kangaroo,
You know I'd hop right up to you,
And if I were an octopus,
I'd thank you, Lord, for my fine looks,
But I just thank you, Father, for making me 'me'.

Chorus

3
If I were a wiggly worm,
I'd thank you, Lord, that I could squirm,
And if I were a billy goat,
I'd thank you, Lord, for my strong throat,
And if I were a fuzzy-wuzzy bear,
I'd thank you, Lord, for my fuzzy-wuzzy hair,
But I just thank you, Father, for making me 'me'.

Chorus

BRIAN HOWARD

10 Think of a world

1
Think of a world without any flowers,
Think of a world without any trees,
Think of a sky without any sunshine,
Think of the air without any breeze.
We thank you, Lord, for flowers and trees and sunshine.
We thank you, Lord, and praise your holy name.

2
Think of the world without any animals,
Think of a field without any herd,
Think of a stream without any fishes,
Think of a dawn without any bird.
We thank you, Lord, for all your living creatures.
We thank you, Lord, and praise your holy name.

3
Think of a world without any science,
Think of a journey with nothing to explore,
Think of a quest without any mystery,
Nothing to seek and nothing left in store.
We thank you, Lord, for miracles of science,
We thank you, Lord, and praise your holy name.

4
Think of a world without any worship,
Think of a God without his only son,
Think of a cross without resurrection,
Only a grave and not a victory won.
We thank you, Lord, for showing us our Saviour,
We thank you, Lord, and praise your holy name.

DOREEN NEWPORT

11 When God made creation

1
When God made creation,
In true adoration,
The stars of the morning all shouted his praise.
The sun in his splendour,
The moon young and tender,
Sang praise to the Lord, the ancient of days.

2
That God loved his children
And happiness willed them,
The stars and the beasts and the flowers knew well;
But wilful man only;
Preferred to be lonely,
And turning from love, to darkness he fell.

3
But God would not leave him
In sorrow and grieving,
And came down to seek him in meekness and love,
And gently he taught him,
And dearly he bought him,
And raised him again to glory above.

4
Then sing of God's glory,
His wonderful story,
O sing out his praise all you children of light;
Through worlds never-ending,
Your praises ascending;
O sing of his love! O sing of his might!

MARGARET ROSE

2
PRAISE AND THANKSGIVING

12 Come and praise the Lord our King

Chorus
Come and praise the Lord our King, Alleluya,
Come and praise the Lord our King, Alleluya.

1
Christ was born in Bethlehem, Alleluya,
Son of God and Son of Man, Alleluya:

Chorus

2
He grew up an earthly child, Alleluya,
Of the world, but undefiled, Alleluya:

Chorus

3
Jesus died at Calvary, Alleluya,
Rose again triumphantly, Alleluya:

Chorus

4
He will cleanse us from our sin, Alleluya,
If we live by faith in him, Alleluya:

Chorus

5
We will live with him one day, Alleluya,
And for ever with him stay, Alleluya:

Chorus

13 God is love

1
God is love: his the care,
Tending each, everywhere,
God is love — all is there.
Jesus came to show him,
That mankind might know him:
Chorus
Sing aloud, loud, loud.
Sing aloud, loud, loud.
God is good. God is truth.
God is beauty. Praise him.
2
None can see God above;
All have here man to love;
Thus may we Godward move,
Finding him in others,
Holding all men brothers:

Chorus

3
Jesus lived here for men,
Strove and died, rose again,
Rules our hearts, now as then;
For he came to save us
By the truth he gave us:

Chorus

4
To our Lord praise we sing —
Light and life, friend and King,
Coming down love to bring
Pattern for our duty,
Showing God in beauty.

Chorus

PERCY DEARMER

14 God of concrete

1
God of concrete, God of steel,
God of piston and of wheel,
God of pylon, God of steam,
God of girder and of beam,
God of atom, God of mine,
All the world of power is thine!

2
Lord of cable, Lord of rail,
Lord of motorway and mail,
Lord of rocket, Lord of flight,
Lord of soaring satellite,
Lord of lightning's livid line,
All the world of speed is thine!

3
Lord of science, Lord of art,
God of map and graph and chart,
Lord of physics and research,
Word of Bible, faith of Church,
Lord of sequence and design,
All the world of truth is thine!

4
God whose glory fills the earth,
Gave the universe its birth,
Loosed the Christ with Easter's might,
Saves the world from evil's blight,
Claims mankind by grace divine,
All the world of love is thine!

RICHARD G JONES

15 Holy, holy, holy!

1
Holy, holy, holy! Lord God Almighty!
Early in the morning our song shall rise to thee;
Holy, holy, holy! Merciful and mighty!
God in three persons, blessèd Trinity!

2
Holy, holy, holy! All the saints adore thee,
Casting down their golden crowns around the glassy sea;
Cherubim and seraphim falling down before thee,
Which wert, and art, and evermore shalt be.

3
Holy, holy, holy! Though the darkness hide thee,
Though the eye of sinful man thy glory may not see,
Only thou art holy, there is none beside thee
Perfect in power, in love, and purity.

4
Holy, holy, holy! Lord God Almighty!
All thy works shall praise thy name, in earth, and sky, and sea;
Holy, holy, holy! Merciful and mighty!
God in three persons, blessèd Trinity!

REGINALD HEBER

16 King of glory, King of peace

1
King of glory, King of peace,
I will love thee;
And that love may never cease,
I will move thee.
Thou hast granted my request,
Thou hast heard me;
Thou didst note my working breast
Thou hast spared me.

2
Wherefore with my utmost art
I will sing thee,
And the cream of all my heart
I will bring thee.
Though my sins against me cried,
Thou didst clear me;
And alone, when they replied,
Thou didst hear me.

3
Seven whole days, not one in seven,
I will praise thee;
In my heart, though not in heaven,
I can raise thee.
Small it is, in this poor sort
To enrol thee:
E'en eternity's too short
To extol thee.

GEORGE HERBERT

17 Mine eyes have seen the glory

1
Mine have seen the glory of the coming of the Lord:
He is trampling out the vintage where the grapes of wrath are stored;
He hath loosed the fateful lightning of his terrible swift sword:
His truth is marching on.

2
I have seen him in the watch-fires of a hundred circling camps;
They have builded him an altar in the evening dews and damps;
I have read his righteous sentence by the dim and flaring lamps:
His day is marching on.

3
He has sounded forth the trumpet that shall never call retreat;
He is sifting out the hearts of men before his judgement-seat;
O, be swift, my soul, to answer him; be jubilant, my feet!
Our God is marching on.

4
In the beauty of the lilies Christ was born across the sea,
With a glory in his bosom that transfigures you and me;
As he died to make men holy, let us live to make men free,
While God is marching on.

5
He is coming like the glory of the morning on the wave;
He is wisdom to the mighty, he is succour to the brave;
So the world shall be his footstool, and the soul of time his slave:
Our God is marching on.

JULIA WARD HOWE

18 Now thank we all our God

1
Now thank we all our God
With heart and hands and voices,
Who wondrous things hath done,
In whom his world rejoices;
Who from our mother's arms
Hath blessed us on our way
With countless gifts of love,
And still is ours today.

2
O may this bounteous God
Through all our life be near us,
With ever-joyful hearts
And blessèd peace to cheer us,
And keep us in his grace,
And guide us when perplexed,
And free us from all ills
In this world and the next.

3
All praise and thanks to God
The Father now be given,
The Son, and him who reigns
With them in highest heaven,
The one eternal God,
Whom earth and heaven adore;
For thus it was, is now,
And shall be evermore.

CATHERINE WINKWORTH

19 O praise ye the Lord!

1
O praise ye the Lord!
Praise him in the height;
Rejoice in his word,
Ye angels of light;
Ye heavens, adore him
By whom ye were made,
And worship before him,
In brightness arrayed.

2
O praise ye the Lord!
Praise him upon earth,
In tuneful accord,
Ye sons of new birth;
Praise him who hath brought you
His grace from above,
Praise him who hath taught you
To sing of his love.

3
O praise ye the Lord,
All things that give sound;
Each jubilant chord,
Re-echo around;
Loud organs, his glory
Forth tell in deep tone,
And sweet harp, the story
Of what he hath done.

4
O praise ye the Lord!
Thanksgiving and song
To him be outpoured
All ages along:
For love in creation,
For heaven restored,
For grace of salvation,
O praise ye the Lord!

HENRY WILLIAMS BAKER

20 Praise, my soul, the King of heaven

1

Praise, my soul, the King of heaven;
To his feet thy tribute bring.
Ransomed, healed, restored, forgiven,
Who, like me, his praise should sing?
Praise him! Praise him! Praise him! Praise him!
Praise the everlasting King.

2

Praise him for his grace and favour
To our fathers in distress;
Praise him still the same for ever,
Slow to chide and swift to bless.
Praise him! Praise him! Praise him! Praise him!
Glorious in his faithfulness.

3

Father-like, he tends and spares us;
Well our feeble frame he knows,
In his hands he gently bears us,
Rescues us from all our foes.
Praise him! Praise him! Praise him! Praise him!
Widely as his mercy flows.

4

Angels, help us to adore him;
Ye behold him face to face;
Sun and moon, bow down before him;
Dwellers all in time and space.
Praise him! Praise him! Praise him! Praise him!
Praise with us the God of grace.

HENRY FRANCIS LYTE

21 Praise the Lord! ye heavens, adore him

1

Praise the Lord! ye heavens, adore him;
Praise him, angels in the height,
Sun and moon, rejoice before him;
Praise him, all ye stars and light.
Praise the Lord, for he hath spoken,
Worlds his mighty voice obeyed;
Laws, which never shall be broken,
For their guidance he hath made.

2

Praise the Lord, for he is glorious:
Never shall his promise fail,
God hath made his saints victorious:
Sin and death shall not prevail,
Praise the God of our salvation;
Hosts on high, his power proclaim;
Heaven and earth, and all creation,
Laud and magnify his name.

22 Rejoice, the Lord is King

1
Rejoice, the Lord is King,
Your Lord and King adore;
Mortals, give thanks and sing,
And triumph evermore:

Chorus
Lift up your heart, lift up your voice;
Rejoice, again I say, rejoice.

2
Jesus, the Saviour, reigns,
The God of truth and love;
When he had purged our stains,
He took his seat above:

Chorus

3
His kingdom cannot fail;
He rules o'er earth and heaven:
The keys of death and hell
Are to our Jesus given:

Chorus

4
He sits at God's right hand
Till all his foes submit,
And bow to his command,
And fall beneath his feet:

Chorus

CHARLES WESLEY

23 Thank you

Thank you for giving me the morning;
Thank you for every day that's new,
Thank you that I can know my worries
Can be cast on you.

2
Thank you for all my friends and brothers;
Thank you for all the men that live,
Thank you for even greatest enemies
I can forgive.

3
Thank you, I have my occupation;
Thank you for every pleasure small,
Thank you for music, light and gladness;
Thank you for them all.

4
Thank you for many little sorrows;
Thank you for every kindly word,
Thank you that everywhere your guidance
Reaches every land.

5
Thank you, I see your word has meaning;
Thank you, I know your spirit here,
Thank you, because you love all people,
Those both far and near.

6
Thank you, O Lord, you spoke unto us;
Thank you that for our words you care,
Thank you, O Lord, you came among us,
Bread and wine to share.

7
Thank you, O Lord, your love is boundless;
Thank you that I am full of you,
Thank you, you made me feel so glad and
Thankful as I do.

MARTIN G SCHNEIDER

3
THE FAMILY OF MAN

24 Better world

1

As I wandered through the city
On a soft September day,
I remembered all the good things
That had helped me on my way,
But among the people round me
Some were sad and some were lonely
And I wished that I could up to them and say:

Chorus

That there's got to be a better world than this,
A world of freedom from anxiety,
Brotherly society,
Where the weak can depend upon the strong,
And you'll know that there's a better world than this,
When you help the people round you
To feel glad that they have found you,
With each little thoughtful deed
For somebody who's in need,
You will build a better world before too long.

2

As I wandered through the city
On a dark and lonely night,
I remembered all the people
Who were longing for the light.
In the shadows lying waiting,
Evil people filled with hating
And I wished that I could up to them and say:
Chorus

3

As I wandered through the city
At the rising of the sun,
I remembered all the children
Whose lives had just begun,
And the people who would guide them,
Hold their hands and stand beside them,
How I wished that I could up to them and say:
Chorus

PETER KNEALE

25 Eternal Father, strong to save

1
Eternal Father, strong to save,
Whose arm hath bound the restless wave,
Who bidd'st the mighty ocean deep
Its own appointed limits keep;
O hear us when we cry to thee
For those in peril on the sea.

2
O Christ, whose voice the waters heard,
And hushed their raging at thy word,
Who walkedst on the foaming deep,
And calm amid the storm didst sleep;
O hear us when we cry to thee
For those in peril on the sea.

3
O save us, God, from storm and tide
On all life's oceans, vast and wide;
Give faith and courage to us most
When drifting from the sheltered coast;
O hear us when we cry to thee
For those in peril on the sea.

4
O Trinity of love and power,
Our brethren shield in danger's hour;
From rock and tempest, fire and foe,
Protect them wheresoe'er they go;
Thus evermore shall rise to thee
Glad hymns of praise from land and sea.

WILLIAM WHITING

26 Far round the world

1
Far round the world thy children sing their song;
From East and West their voices sweetly blend,
Praising the Lord, in whom young lives are strong,
Jesus our guide, our hero and our friend.

2
Where thy wide ocean, wave on rolling wave,
Beats through the ages, on each island shore,
They praise their Lord, whose hand alone can save,
Whose sea of love surrounds them evermore.

3
Still there are lands where none have seen thy face,
Children whose hearts have never shared thy joy;
Yet thou wouldst pour on these thy radiant grace,
Give thy glad strength to every girl and boy.

4
All round the world let children sing thy song;
From East and West their voices sweetly blend,
Praising the Lord in whom young lives are strong,
Jesus our guide, our hero, and our friend.

BASIL J MATHEWS

27 He's got the whole world in his hands

Chorus
He's got the whole world in his hands,
He's got the whole wide world in his hands,
He's got the whole world in his hands,
He's got the whole world in his hands.

1
He's got the wind and the rain in his hands,
He's got the wind and the rain in his hands,
He's got the wind and the rain in his hands,
He's got the whole world in his hands.

Chorus

2
He's got the sun and the moon in his hands,
He's got the sun and the moon in his hands,
He's got the sun and the moon in his hands,
He's got the whole world in his hands.

Chorus

3
He's got you and me brother in his hands,
He's got you and me brother in his hands,
He's got you and me brother in his hands,
He's got the whole world in his hands.

Chorus

4
He's got everybody here in his hands,
He's got everybody here in his hands,
He's got everybody here in his hands,
He's got the whole world in his hands.

Chorus

28 I belong to a family

1
I belong to a family, the biggest on earth,
Ten thousand every day are coming to birth,
Our name isn't Davies, or Groves or Jones,
It's the name every man should be proud he owns:

Chorus
It's the family of man, keeps growing,
The family of man, keeps sowing
The seeds of a new life every day.

2
I've got a sister in Melbourne, a brother in Paree,
The whole wide world is mum and dad to me,
Wherever you turn you will find my kin,
Whatever the creed or the colour of skin.

Chorus

3
The miner in the Rhondda, the coolie in Peking,
Men across the world who reap and plough and spin,
They've got a life and others to share it,
Let's bridge the oceans and declare it:

Chorus

4
Some people say the world is a horrible place,
But it's just as good or bad as the human race;
Dirt and misery or health and joy,
Man can build or can destroy:

Chorus

KARL DALLAS

29 If I had a hammer

1
If I had a hammer, I'd hammer in the morning,
I'd hammer in the evening, all over this land;
I'd hammer out danger, I'd hammer out a warning,
I'd hammer out love between my brothers and my sisters,
All over this land.

2
If I had a bell, I'd ring it in the morning,
I'd ring it in the evening, all over this land;
I'd ring out danger, I'd ring out a warning,
I'd ring out love between my brothers and my sisters,
All over this land.

3
If I had a song, I'd sing it in the morning,
I'd sing it in the evening, all over this land;
I'd sing out danger, I'd sing out a warning,
I'd sing out love between my brothers and my sisters,
All over this land.

4
Well I've got a hammer, and I've got a bell,
And I've got a song to sing all over this land;
It's the hammer of justice, it's the bell of freedom,
It's the song about love between my brothers and my sisters,
All over this land.

LEE HAYS AND PETE SEEGER

30 If you keep a promise

1
If you keep a promise,
You will keep a friend,
Others learn to trust you
To the very end.
If you help a stranger,
Showing that you care,
Happiness will follow
And your friendship share.
Happiness will follow
And your friendship share.

2
If you keep a promise,
If your word is true,
Others will not doubt you
In the things you do.
When we wake from sleeping
And see the morning light,
We believe God's promise
That day will follow night.
We believe God's promise
Day will follow night.

3
If you keep a promise,
You will keep a friend,
Others learn to trust you
To the very end.
If promises are broken
And your plans fall through,
Put your trust in someone
Who died for me and you.
Put your trust in one
Who died for me and you.

HAROLD CLARKE

31 In Christ there is no East or West

1
In Christ there is no East or West,
In him no South or North,
But one great fellowship of love
Throughout the whole wide earth.

2
In him shall true hearts everywhere
Their high communion find,
His service is the golden cord
Close-binding all mankind.

3
Join hands, then, brothers of the faith,
Whate'er your race may be!
Who serves my Father as a son
Is surely kin to me.

4
In Christ now meet both East and West,
In him meet South and North,
All Christly souls are one in him,
Throughout the whole wide earth.

JOHN OXENHAM

32 Kum ba yah

1
Kum ba yah, my Lord, Kum ba yah,
Kum ba yah, my Lord, Kum ba yah,
Kum ba yah, my Lord, Kum ba yah,
O Lord, Kum ba yah.

2
Someone's waiting, Lord, Kum ba yah,
Someone's waiting, Lord, Kum ba yah,
Someone's waiting, Lord, Kum ba yah,
O Lord, Kum ba yah.

3
Someone's crying, Lord, Kum ba yah,
Someone's crying, Lord, Kum ba yah,
Someone's crying, Lord, Kum ba yah,
O Lord, Kum ba yah.

4
Someone's singing, Lord, Kum ba yah,
Someone's singing, Lord, Kum ba yah,
Someone's singing, Lord, Kum ba yah,
O Lord, Kum ba yah.

5
Someone's praying, Lord, Kum ba yah,
Someone's praying, Lord, Kum ba yah,
Someone's praying, Lord, Kum ba yah,
O Lord, Kum ba yah.

33 Let all the world in every corner sing

1
Let all the world in every corner sing:
My God and King.
The heavens are not too high,
His praise may thither fly;
The earth is not too low,
His praises there may grow.
Let all the world in every corner sing:
My God and King!

2
Let all the world in every corner sing:
My God and King.
The Church with psalms must shout,
No door can keep them out;
But, above all, the heart
Must bear the longest part.
Let all the world in every corner sing:
My God and King!

GEORGE HERBERT

34 Life is better

1
Life is better, life is fair,
When we always try to share;
How much sweeter life can be
When we're living in harmony.

Chorus
Harmony, all agree,
Harmony for you and me,
Harmony, all agree,
All pull together in harmony.

2
See the other point of view,
Serving God and being true,
He will always see us through
If we're living in harmony.

Chorus

3
Children's voices raised in sound,
Mighty engines whirring round,
Happy concord may be found
When we're working in harmony.

Chorus

4
Each one matters, weak and strong,
Team work helps the game along;
Peace on earth will not take long
If we're working in harmony.

Chorus

HAROLD CLARKE

35 Love is something

Chorus

Love is something if you give it away,
Give it away, give it away.
Love is something if you give it away,
You end up having more.

1

It's just like a magic penny;
Hold it tight and you won't have any;
Lend it, spend it, and you'll have so many,
They'll roll all over the floor, for

Chorus

2

So let's go dancing till the break of day.
And if there's a piper, we can pay.
For love is something if you give it away,
You end up having more.

Chorus

MALVINA REYNOLDS

36 Summer suns are glowing

1
Summer suns are glowing
Over land and sea,
Happy light is flowing
Bountiful and free,
Everything rejoices
In the mellow rays,
All earth's thousand voices
Swell the psalm of praise.

2
God's free mercy streameth
Over all the world,
And his banner gleameth
Everywhere unfurled.
Broad and deep and glorious
As the heaven above,
Shines in might victorious
His eternal love.

3
Lord, upon our blindness
Thy pure radiance pour;
For thy loving kindness
Make us love thee more.
And when clouds are drifting
Dark across our sky,
Then, the veil uplifting,
Father, be thou nigh.

4
We will never doubt thee,
Though thou veil thy light:
Life is dark without thee;
Death with thee is bright.
Light of light, shine o'er us
On our pilgrim way,
Go thou still before us
To the endless day.

WILLIAM WALSHAM HOW

37 Take care to wonder

Chorus
Take care to wonder
At the world through which you wander,
Never hurry by an open door;
For you live in a universe
Full of miracles galore.

1
Look for God in small things,
Drops of rain or a grain of sand;
Praise him whenever you find him
In anything small.

Chorus

2
Look for God in weak things,
New-born deer or a tearful child;
Praise him whenever you find him
In anything weak.

Chorus

3
Look for God in bright things,
Someone's eyes or the skies at noon
Praise him whenever you find him
In anything bright.

Chorus

4
Look for God in black things,
Storms at dusk or a brother's skin;
Praise him whenever you find him
In anything black.

Chorus

5
Look for God in kind things,
Parents' love or a doctor's care;
Praise him whenever you find him
In anyone kind.

Chorus

38 The ink is black

1
The ink is black, the page is white,
Together we learn to read and write,
To read and write.
And now a child can understand,
This is the law of all the land,
All the land!
The ink is black, the page is white,
Together we learn to read and write,
To read and write.

2

The board is black, the chalk is white,
The words stand out so clear and bright,
So clear and bright.
And now at last we plainly see
The alphabet of liberty,
Liberty!
The board is black, the chalk is white,
The words stand out so clear and bright,
So clear and bright.

3

A child is black, a child is white,
The whole world looks upon the sight,
A beautiful sight.
For very well the whole world knows,
This is the way that freedom grows,
Freedom grows!
A child is black, a child is white,
The whole world looks upon the sight,
A beautiful sight.

4

The world is black, the world is white,
It turns by day and it turns by night.
It turns by night.
It turns so each and every one
Can take his station in the sun,
In the sun!
The world is black, the world is white,
It turns by day and it turns by night,
It turns by night.

DAVID ARKIN

39 When I needed a neighbour

1
When I needed a neighbour, were you there, were you there?
When I needed a neighbour, were you there?
Chorus
And the creed and the colour and the name won't matter,
Were you there?

2
I was hungry and thirsty, were you there, were you there?
I was hungry and thirsty, were you there?

Chorus

3
I was cold, I was naked, were you there, were you there?
I was cold, I was naked, were you there?

Chorus

4
When I needed a shelter, were you there, were you there?
When I needed a shelter, were you there?

Chorus

5
When I needed a healer, were you there, were you there?
When I needed a healer, were you there?

Chorus

6
Wherever you travel, I'll be there, I'll be there,
Wherever you travel, I'll be there.

Chorus

SYDNEY CARTER

40 Cross over the road

1
Would you walk by on the other side,
When someone called for aid?
Would you walk by on the other side,
And would you be afraid?

Chorus
Cross over the road, my friend,
Ask the Lord his strength to lend,
His compassion has no end,
Cross over the road.

2
Would you walk by on the other side,
When you saw a loved one stray?
Would you walk by on the other side,
Or would you watch and pray?

Chorus

3
Would you walk by on the other side,
When starving children cried?
Would you walk by on the other side
And would you not provide?

Chorus

PAMELA VERRALL

4
OUR DAILY LIFE

41 Amazing grace

1
Amazing grace! How sweet the sound
That saved a wretch like me!
I once was lost, but now am found,
Was blind, but now I see.

2
'Twas grace that taught my heart to fear,
And grace my fears relieved;
How precious did that grace appear
The hour I first believed.

3
Thro' many dangers, toils, and snares
I have already come;
'Tis grace hath brought me safe thus far,
And grace will lead me home.

4
The Lord has promised good to me,
His word my hope secures;
He will my shield and portion be
As long as life endures.

JOHN NEWTON

42 Colours of day

1
Colours of day dawn into the mind,
The sun has come up, the night is behind.
Go down in the city, into the street,
And let's give the message to the people we meet.

Chorus
So light up the fire and let the flame burn,
Open the door, let Jesus return.
Take seeds of his Spirit, let the fruit grow,
Tell the people of Jesus, let his love show.

2
Go through the park, on into the town;
The sun still shines on, it never goes down.
The light of the world is risen again;
The people of darkness are needing our friend.

Chorus

3
Open your eyes, look into the sky,
The darkness has come, the sun came to die.
The evening draws on, the sun disappears,
But Jesus is living, and his Spirit is near.

Chorus

SUE McCLELLAN, JOHN PAC and KEITH RYECROFT

43 Father, hear the prayer we offer

1
Father, hear the prayer we offer;
Not for ease that prayer shall be,
But for strength that we may ever
Live our lives courageously.

2
Not for ever in green pastures
Do we ask our way to be;
But the steep and rugged pathway
May we tread rejoicingly.

3
Not for ever by still waters
Would we idly rest and stay;
But would smite the living fountains
From the rocks along our way.

4
Be our strength in hours of weakness,
In our wanderings be our guide;
Through endeavour, failure, danger,
Father, be thou at our side.

MRS L M WILLIS

44 Give me joy in my heart

1
Give me joy in my heart, keep me praising,
Give me joy in my heart, I pray;
Give me joy in my heart, keep me praising,
Keep me praising till the break of day:

Chorus
Sing Hosanna! Sing Hosanna!
Sing Hosanna to the King of Kings!
Sing Hosanna! Sing Hosanna!
Sing Hosanna to the King.

2
Give me peace in my heart, keep me loving,
Give me peace in my heart, I pray;
Give me peace in my heart, keep me loving,
Keep me loving till the break of day:

Chorus

3
Give me love in my heart, keep me serving,
Give me love in my heart, I pray;
Give me love in my heart, keep me serving,
Keep me serving till the break of day:

Chorus

45 God give me ears

1
God give me ears
That will always hear thee,
God give me eyes
That will see far and wide;
God give me hands
That will bring beauty near me,
God give me feet
That will walk by thy side;
God give me ears
That will always hear thee,
God give me eyes
That will see far and wide.

2
God fill my thoughts
With the spirit of seeking,
Visions of wonder
Let me ever see;
Give to my tongue
Only truth when I'm speaking,
Fill my heart
With the knowledge of thee;
God fill my thoughts
With the spirit of seeking,
Visions of wonder
Let me ever see.

46 He who would valiant be

1
He who would valiant be
'Gainst all disaster,
Let him in constancy
Follow the Master.
There's no discouragement
Shall make him once relent
His first avowed intent
To be a pilgrim.

2
Who so beset him round
With dismal stories,
Do but themselves confound —
His strength the more is.
No foes shall stay his might,
Though he with giants fight:
He will make good his right
To be a pilgrim.

3
Since, Lord, thou dost defend
Us with thy spirit,
We know we at the end
Shall life inherit.
Then fancies flee away!
I'll fear not what men say,
I'll labour night and day
To be a pilgrim.

P DEARMER (AFTER JOHN BUNYAN)

47 Heavenly Father

1
Heavenly Father, may thy blessing
Rest upon thy children now,
When in praise thy name they hallow,
When in prayer to thee they bow:
In the wondrous story reading
Of the Lord of truth and grace,
May they see thy love reflected
In the light of his dear face.

2
May they learn from this great story
All the arts of friendliness;
Truthful speech and honest action,
Courage, patience, steadfastness;
How to master self and temper,
How to make their conduct fair;
When to speak and when be silent,
When to do and when forbear.

3
May his spirit wise and holy
With his gifts their spirits bless,
Make them loving, joyous, peaceful,
Rich in goodness, gentleness,
Strong in self-control, and faithful,
Kind in thought and deed; for he
Sayeth, 'What ye do for others
Ye are doing unto me.'

W CHARTER PIGGOTT

48 I sing a song of the saints of God

1
I sing a song of the saints of God,
Patient and brave and true,
Who toiled and fought and lived and died
For the Lord they loved and knew.
And one was a doctor, and one was a queen,
And one was a shepherdess on the green:
They were all of them saints of God; and I mean,
God helping, to be one too.

2
They loved their Lord so good and dear,
And his love made them strong;
And they followed the right, for Jesu's sake,
The whole of their good lives long.
And one was a soldier, and one was a priest,
And one was slain by a fierce wild beast:
And there's not any reason, no, not the least,
Why I shouldn't be one too.

3
They lived not only in ages past,
There are hundreds of thousands still;
The world is bright with the joyous saints
Who love to do Jesu's will.
You can meet them in school, or in lanes, or at sea,
In church, or in trains, or in shops, or at tea,
For the saints of God began just like me,
And I mean to be one too.

LESBIA SCOTT

49 Just as I am

1
Just as I am, thine own to be,
Friend of the young, who lovest me,
To consecrate myself to thee,
O Jesus Christ, I come.

2
In the glad morning of my day
My life to give, my vows to pay,
With no reserve and no delay,
With all my heart I come.

3
I would live ever in the light,
I would work ever for the right,
I would serve thee with all my might,
Therefore to thee I come.

4
Just as I am, young, strong and free,
To be the best that I can be
For truth, and righteousness, and thee,
Lord of my life, I come.

5
Just as I am, thine own to be,
Friend of the young, who lovest me,
To consecrate myself to thee,
O Jesus Christ, I come.

MARIANNE FARNINGHAM

50 Life is great!

1
Life is great! So sing about it,
As we can and as we should —
Shops and buses, towns and people,
Village, farmlands, field and wood.
Life is great and life is given.
Life is lovely, free and good.

2
Life is great! Whatever happens,
Snow or sunshine, joy or pain,
Hardship, grief or disillusion,
Suffering that I can't explain —
Life is great if someone loves me,
Holds my hand and calls my name.

3
Love is giving and receiving —
Boy and girl, or friend with friend.
Love is bearing and forgiving,
All the hurts that hate can send.
Love's the greatest way of living,
Hoping, trusting, to the end.

4
God is great! In Christ he loved us,
As we should but never can —
Love that suffered, hoped and trusted,
When disciples turned and ran,
Love that broke through death for ever —
Praise that loving, living man!

One verse omitted BRIAN WREN

51 Lord of all hopefulness

1
Lord of all hopefulness, Lord of all joy,
Whose trust, ever child-like, no cares could destroy,
Be there at our waking, and give us, we pray
Your bliss in our hearts, Lord, at the break of the day.

2
Lord of all eagerness, Lord of all faith,
Whose strong hands were skilled at the plane and the lathe,
Be there at our labours, and give us, we pray,
Your strength in our hearts, Lord, at the noon of the day.

3
Lord of all kindliness, Lord of all grace,
Your hands swift to welcome, your arms to embrace,
Be there at our homing, and give us we pray,
Your love in our hearts, Lord, at the eve of the day.

4
Lord of all gentleness, Lord of all calm,
Whose voice is contentment, whose presence is balm,
Be there at our sleeping, and give us, we pray,
Your peace in our hearts, Lord, at the end of the day.

JAN STRUTHER

52 New every morning

1
New every morning is the love
Our wakening and uprising prove;
Through sleep and darkness safely brought,
Restored to life, and power, and thought.

2
New mercies, each returning day,
Hover around us while we pray;
New perils past, new sins forgiven,
New thoughts of God, new hopes of heaven.

3
If on our daily course our mind
Be set to hallow all we find,
New treasures still, of countless price,
God will provide for sacrifice.

4
The trivial round, the common task,
Will furnish all we ought to ask,
Room to deny ourselves, a road
To bring us daily nearer God.

5
Only, O Lord, in thy dear love
Fit us for perfect rest above;
And help us this and every day
To live more nearly as we pray.

JOHN KEBLE

53 O Jesus, I have promised

1

O Jesus, I have promised
To serve thee to the end;
Be thou for ever near me,
My master and my friend;
I shall not fear the battle
If thou art by my side,
Nor wander from the pathway
If thou wilt be my guide.

2

O Jesus, thou hast promised
To all who follow thee,
That where thou art in glory
There shall thy servant be;
And, Jesus, I have promised
To serve thee to the end;
O give me grace to follow
My master and my friend.

3

O let me see thy foot-marks
And in them plant mine own;
My hope to follow duly
Is in thy strength alone;
O guide me, call me, draw me,
Uphold me to the end;
And then in heaven receive me,
My Saviour and my friend.

JOHN ERNEST BODE

54 One more step along the world I go

1
One more step along the world I go,
One more step along the world I go,
From the old things to the new
Keep me travelling along with you.
Chorus
And it's from the old I travel to the new,
Keep me travelling along with you.

2
Round the corners of the world I turn,
More and more about the world I learn.
And the new things that I see
You'll be looking at along with me.
Chorus

3
As I travel through the bad and good
Keep me travelling the way I should.
Where I see no way to go
You'll be telling me the way, I know.
Chorus

4
Give me courage when the world is rough,
Keep me loving though the world is tough.
Leap and sing in all I do,
Keep me travelling along with you.
Chorus

5
You are older than the world can be
You are younger than the life in me.
Ever old and ever new,
Keep me travelling along with you.
Chorus

SYDNEY CARTER

55 Onward, Christian soldiers

1
Onward, Christian soldiers,
Marching as to war,
With the cross of Jesus
Going on before!
Christ, the royal Master,
Leads against the foe;
Forward into battle,
See, his banners go:

Chorus
Onward, Christian soldiers,
Marching as to war,
With the cross of Jesus
Going on before.

2
Crowns and thrones may perish,
Kingdoms rise and wane,
But the Church of Jesus
Constant will remain;
Gates of hell can never
'Gainst that Church prevail;
We have Christ's own promise,
And that cannot fail:

Chorus

3
Onward, then, ye people,
Join the happy throng;
Blend with us your voices
In the triumph song;
Glory, laud and honour
Unto Christ the King;
This through countless ages
Men and angels sing:

Chorus

S BARING-GOULD

56 Our Father

1
Our Father who art in heaven,
Hallowed be thy name,
Thy kingdom come, thy will be done,
Hallowed be thy name.

2
On the earth as it is in heaven,
Hallowed be thy name,
Give us this day our daily bread,
Hallowed be thy name.

3
And forgive us all our trespasses,
Hallowed be thy name.
As we forgive those who trespass against us,
Hallowed be thy name.

4
And lead us not into temptation,
Hallowed be thy name.
But deliver us from all that is evil,
Hallowed be thy name.

5
For thine is the kingdom, the power and the glory,
Hallowed be thy name.
For ever and for ever and ever,
Hallowed be thy name.

6
Amen, Amen, it shall be so,
Hallowed be thy name.
Amen, Amen, it shall be so,
Hallowed be thy name.

57 Show me a way

1
Show me a way of loving and living,
How to be cheerful, kind and forgiving,
Leading my life in my work and my thought and my play.

Chorus
As with love in my heart
I can make a fresh start every day.
Yes with love in my heart
I can make a fresh start every day.

2
Show me persistence in trusting and trying,
Keep me from grumbling, complaining or sighing,
Never discouraged by failure or doubt or dismay.

Chorus

3
Show me the way to be useful and grateful,
Smother all thoughts which are harmful or hateful,
Guiding me back on the track if I wander or stray.

Chorus

HAROLD CLARKE

58 Soldiers of Christ, arise

1
Soldiers of Christ, arise,
And put your armour on;
Strong in the strength which God supplies,
Through his eternal son;
Strong in the Lord of Hosts,
And in his mighty power;
Who in the strength of Jesus trusts
Is more than conqueror.

2
Stand then in his great might,
With all his strength endued;
And take, to arm you for the fight,
The panoply of God.
To keep your armour bright
Attend with constant care,
Still walking in your captain's sight,
And watching unto prayer.

3
From strength to strength go on,
Wrestle, and fight, and pray;
Tread all the powers of darkness down,
And win the well-fought day.
That having all things done,
And all your conflicts past,
Ye may o'ercome, through Christ alone,
And stand entire at last.

CHARLES WESLEY

59 The Lord's my shepherd

1
The Lord's my shepherd, I'll not want.
He makes me down to lie
In pastures green: he leadeth me
The quiet waters by.

2
My soul he doth restore again,
And me to walk doth make
Within the paths of righteousness,
E'en for his own name's sake.

3
Yea, though I walk in death's dark vale,
Yet will I fear no ill:
For thou art with me, and thy rod
And staff me comfort still.

4
My table thou hast furnished
In presence of my foes;
My head thou dost with oil anoint,
And my cup overflows.

5
Goodness and mercy all my life
Shall surely follow me:
And in God's house for evermore
My dwelling-place shall be.

FRANCIS ROUS

60 Travelling

1
With Christ by our side
To act as our guide,
We can journey along on life's way,
He makes us as bold
As the travellers of old,
Day after day after day,
Day after day after day.

2
Our courage is strong
As we travel along,
With highways and hillsides to climb;
Through the clouds and the rain
He guides us again,
Time after time after time,
Time after time after time.

3
At each corner we turn,
There is something to learn,
No pausing for doubt or delay;
As we travel life's road,
He can lighten our load,
Day after day after day
Day after day after day.

4
A beam burning bright,
Like a torch in the night,
For Christ is the light and the sign;
For we know, as we grow,
The way he will show,
Time after time after time,
Time after time after time.

5
So with Christ by our side,
To act as our guide,
Let us journey along on life's way;
In each hour that we spend
Keep us wise till the end,
Day after day after day,
Day after day after day.

HAROLD CLARKE

61 When a knight won his spurs

1
When a knight won his spurs, in the stories of old,
He was gentle and brave, he was gallant and bold,
With a shield on his arm and a lance in his hand,
For God and for valour he rode through the land.

2
No charger have I, and no sword by my side,
Yet still to adventure and battle I ride,
Though back into storyland giants have fled,
And the knights are no more and the dragons are dead.

3
Let faith be my shield and let joy be my steed
'Gainst the dragons of anger, the ogres of greed;
And let me set free, with the sword of my youth,
From the castle of darkness the power of the truth.

JAN STRUTHER

5
LORD JESUS CHRIST

62 Alleluya, sing to Jesus

1
Alleluya, sing to Jesus,
His the sceptre, his the throne;
Alleluya, his the triumph,
His the victory alone:
Hark! The songs of peaceful Sion
Thunder like a mighty flood;
Jesus, out of every nation,
Hath redeemed us by his blood.

2
Alleluya, not as orphans
Are we left in sorrow now;
Alleluya, he is near us,
Faith believes, nor questions how;
Though the cloud from sight received him
When the forty days were o'er,
Shall our hearts forget his promise,
'I am with you evermore'?

3
Alleluya, Alleluya,
Glory be to God on high;
To the Father, and the Saviour,
Who has gained the victory;
Glory to the Holy Spirit,
Fount of love and sanctity;
Alleluya, Alleluya,
To the triune Majesty.

W CHATTERTON DIX

63 At the name of Jesus

1
At the name of Jesus
Every knee shall bow,
Every tongue confess him
King of glory now;
'Tis the Father's pleasure
We should call him Lord,
Who from the beginning
Was the mighty word.

2
Humbled for a season,
To receive a name
From the lips of sinners
Unto whom he came,
Faithfully he bore it
Spotless to the last,
Brought it back victorious
When from death he passed.

3
Name him, brothers, name him,
With love as strong as death,
But with awe and wonder,
And with bated breath;
He is God and Saviour,
He is Christ the Lord,
Ever to be worshipped,
Trusted and adored.

4
In your hearts enthrone him;
There let him subdue
All that is not holy,
All that is not true:
Crown him as your captain
In temptations's hour;
Let his will enfold you
In its light and power.

CAROLINE M NOEL

64 Counting, counting

1
Counting, counting, the pebbles by the sea;
Counting, counting, the apples on a tree;
Counting, counting, the seconds ticking by;
Counting, counting, the stars in the sky.

2
One for Jesus, the name above all names;
Two for brothers, remember John and James?
Three for the wise men, to Bethlehem proceed;
Four for the gospels, the stories we should read.

3
Five for feeding, five loaves, five thousand fed;
Six for making, six days the earth was made;
Seven for the people, with Noah in the ark;
Eight for the candles, all brightness in the dark.

4
Nine for Christian, the letters in that name;
Ten for promise, the laws from Moses came;
Eleven stars a-shining, as Joseph dreamed one night;
Twelve brave disciples who saw the son of light.

5
Counting, counting, the pebbles by the sea;
Counting, counting, the apples on a tree;
Counting, counting, the seconds ticking by;
Counting, counting, the stars in the sky.

HAROLD CLARKE

65 Go, tell it on the mountain

Chorus
Go, tell it on the mountain,
Over the hills and everywhere;
Go, tell it on the mountain
That Jesus Christ is born!

1
While shepherds kept their watching o'er wand'ring flocks by night,
Behold from out of heaven there shone a holy light.

Chorus

2
And lo, when they had seen it, they all bowed down and prayed,
They travelled on together to where the Babe was laid.

Chorus

3
When I was a seeker, I sought both night and day:
I asked the Lord to help me and he showed me the way . . .

Chorus

66 I saw the grass

1

I saw the grass, I saw the trees
And the boats along the shore.
I saw the shapes of many things
I had only sensed before.
And I saw the faces of men more clearly
Than if I had never been blind,
The lines of envy around their lips
And the greed and the hate in their eyes.
And I turned away, yes, I turned away,
For I had seen the perfect face of a real and proper man,
The man who'd brought me from the
Dark into light, where life began.

2

I hurried then away from town
To a quiet, lonely place.
I found a clear, unruffled pool
And I gazed upon my face.
And I saw the image of me more clearly
Than if I had never been blind,
The lines of envy around the lips
And the greed and the hate in the eyes.
And I turned away, yes, I turned away,
For I had seen the perfect face of a real and proper man,
The man who'd brought me from the
Dark into light, where life began.

3
I made my way into the town,
To the busy, crowded streets,
The shops and stalls and alley-ways,
To the squalor and the heat.
And I saw the faces of men more clearly
Than if I had never been blind,
The lines of sorrow around their lips
And the child looking out from their eyes.
And I turned to them, yes, I turned to them,
Remembering the perfect face of a real and proper man,
The man who'd brought me from the
Dark into light, where life began.

ESTELLE WHITE

67 It fell upon a summer's day

1
It fell upon a summer's day,
When Jesus walked in Galilee,
The mothers from a village brought
Their children to his knee.

2
He took them in his arms, and laid
His hands on each remembered head;
'Suffer these little ones to come
To me,' he gently said.

3
'Forbid them not; unless ye bear
The childlike heart your hearts within,
Unto my kingdom ye may come,
But may not enter in.'

4
Master, I fain would enter there;
O let me follow thee, and share
Thy meek and lowly heart, and be
Freed from all worldly care.

STOPFORD AUGUSTUS BROOKE

68 Jesus, good above all other

1
Jesus, good above all other,
Gentle child of gentle mother,
In a stable-born our brother,
Give us grace to persevere.

2
Jesus, cradled in a manger,
For us facing every danger,
Living as a homeless stranger,
Make we thee our King most dear.

3
Jesus, for thy people dying,
Risen Master, death defying,
Lord in heaven, thy grace supplying,
Keep us to thy presence near.

4
Jesus, who our sorrows bearest,
All our thoughts and hopes thou sharest,
Thou to man the truth declarest;
Help us all thy truth to hear.

5
Lord, in all our doings guide us;
Pride and hate shall ne'er divide us;
We'll go on with thee beside us,
And with joy we'll persevere!

P DEARMER

69 Jesu's hands were kind hands

1
Jesu's hands were kind hands, doing good to all,
Healing pain and sickness, blessing children small;
Washing tired feet and saving those who fall.
Jesu's hands were kind hands, doing good to all.

2
Take my hands, Lord Jesus, let them work for you.
Make them strong and gentle, kind in all I do.
Let me watch you, Jesus, till I'm gentle too;
Till my hands are kind hands, quick to work for you.

3
Take my feet, Lord Jesus, let them run for you,
Quick to be of service, swift in all I do.
Take my voice and use it, help me to be true;
Take my life, Lord Jesus, doing all for you.

MARGARET CROPPER

70 Lord of the Dance

1
I danced in the morning
When the world was begun,
And I danced in the moon
And the stars and the sun;
And I came down from Heaven
And I danced on the earth,
At Bethlehem
I had my birth.

Chorus
Dance then, wherever you may be,
I am the Lord of the Dance, said he,
And I'll lead you all wherever you may be,
And I'll lead you all in the Dance, said he.

2
I danced for the scribe
And the pharisee,
But they would not dance
And they wouldn't follow me.
I danced for the fishermen,
For James and John —
They came with me
And the dance went on.
Chorus

3
I danced on the Sabbath
And I cured the lame;
The holy people
Said it was a shame.
They whipped and they stripped
And they hung me on high,
And they left me there
On a Cross to die.
Chorus

4
I danced on a Friday
When the sky turned black —
It's hard to dance
With the devil on your back.
They buried my body
And they thought I'd gone,
But I am the dance,
And I still go on.
Chorus

5
They cut me down
And I leapt up high;
I am the life
That'll never, never die;
I'll live in you
If you'll live in me —
I am the Lord
Of the Dance, said he.
Chorus

SYDNEY CARTER

71 Lord Jesus Christ

1
Lord Jesus Christ, you have come to us,
You are one with us, Mary's son.
Cleansing our souls from all their sin,
Pouring your love and goodness in,
Jesus our love for you we sing,
Living Lord.

2
Lord Jesus Christ, now and every day
Teach us how to pray, son of God.
You have commanded us to do
This in remembrance, Lord, of you:
Into our lives your power breaks through,
Living Lord.

3
Lord Jesus Christ, you have come to us,
Born as one of us,
Mary's son.
Led out to die on Calvary,
Risen from death to set us free,
Living Lord Jesus, help us see
You are Lord.

4
Lord Jesus Christ, I would come to you,
Live my life for you,
Son of God.
All your commands I know are true,
Your many gifts will make me new,
Into my life your power breaks through,
Living Lord.

PATRICK APPLEFORD

72 My song is love unknown

1
My song is love unknown,
My Saviour's love to me,
Love to the loveless shown,
That they might lovely be.
O who am I,
That for my sake
My Lord should take
Frail flesh, and die?

2
Sometimes they strew his way,
And his sweet praises sing;
Resounding all the day
Hosannas to their King.
Then 'Crucify!'
Is all their breath,
And for his death
They thirst and cry.

3
Why, what hath my Lord done?
What makes this rage and spite?
He made the lame to run,
He gave the blind their sight.
Sweet injuries!
Yet they at these
Themselves displease,
And 'gainst him rise.

4
Here might I stay and sing,
No story so divine;
Never was love, dear King,
Never was grief like thine.
This is my friend,
In whose sweet praise
I all my days
Could gladly spend.

SAMUEL CROSSMAN

73 Seek ye first

1
Seek ye first the kingdom of God,
And his righteousness,
And all these things shall be added unto you;
Allelu, alleluya.

Chorus
Alleluya, alleluya,
Alleluya, allelu, alleluya

2
Man cannot live by bread alone
But by every word
That proceeds from the mouth of God.
Allelu, alleluya.

Chorus

3
Ask and it shall be given unto you,
Seek and ye shall find,
Knock and the door shall be opened unto you.
Allelu, alleluya.

Chorus

74 Were you there?

1
Were you there when they crucified my Lord?
Were you there when they crucified my Lord?
O! Sometimes it causes me to tremble, tremble, tremble.
Were you there when they crucified my Lord?

2
Were you there when they nailed him to the tree?
Were you there when they nailed him to the tree?
O! Sometimes it causes me to tremble, tremble, tremble.
Were you there when they nailed him to the tree?

3
Were you there when they laid him in the tomb?
Were you there when they laid him in the tomb?
O! Sometimes it causes me to tremble, tremble, tremble.
Were you there when they laid him in the tomb?

4
Were you there when they rolled away the stone?
Were you there when they rolled away the stone?
O! Sometimes it causes me to tremble, tremble, tremble.
Were you there when they rolled away the stone?

6
FESTIVAL AND CELEBRATION

75 All glory, laud, and honour

Chorus
All glory, laud, and honour
To thee, Redeemer, King,
To whom the lips of children
Made sweet hosannas ring.

1
Thou art the King of Israel,
Thou David's royal son,
Who in the Lord's name comest,
The King and blessèd one:

Chorus

2
The company of angels
Are praising thee on high,
And mortal men and all things
Created make reply:

Chorus

3
The people of the Hebrews
With palms before thee went;
Our praise and prayer and anthems
Before thee we present:

Chorus

ST THEODULPH OF ORLEANS TRANS. BY J M NEALE

76 Come, ye thankful people, come

1

Come, ye thankful people, come,
Raise the song of harvest home!
All is safely gathered in,
Ere the winter storms begin;
God, our Maker, doth provide
For our wants to be supplied;
Come to God's own temple, come;
Raise the song of harvest home!

2

All this world is God's own field,
Fruit unto his praise to yield;
Wheat and tares together sown,
Unto joy or sorrow grown;
First the blade and then the ear,
Then the full corn shall appear:
Lord of harvest, grant that we
Wholesome grain and pure may be.

3

Even so, Lord, quickly come;
Bring thy final harvest home:
Gather thou thy people in,
Free from sorrow, free from sin;
There, for ever purified,
In thy garner to abide:
Come, with all thine angels, come,
Raise the glorious harvest home!

H ALFORD

77 God whose farm is all creation

1
God whose farm is all creation,
Take the gratitude we give;
Take the finest of our harvest,
Crops we grow that men may live.

2
Take our ploughing, seeding, reaping,
Hopes and fears of sun and rain,
All our thinking, planning, waiting
Ripened in this fruit and grain.

3
All our labour, all our watching,
All our calendar of care,
In these crops of your creation
Take, O God: they are our prayer.

JOHN ARLOTT

78 Hark the glad sound!

1
Hark the glad sound! the Saviour comes,
The Saviour promised long!
Let every heart prepare a throne,
And every voice a song.

2
He comes the prisoners to release
In Satan's bondage held;
The gates of brass before him burst,
The iron fetters yield.

3
He comes the broken heart to bind,
The bleeding soul to cure,
And with the treasures of his grace
To enrich the humble poor.

4
Our glad Hosannas, Prince of Peace,
Thy welcome shall proclaim;
And heaven's eternal arches ring
With thy belovèd name.

P DODDRIDGE

79 Holy Spirit, hear us

1
Holy Spirit, hear us;
Help us while we sing;
Breathe into the music
Of the praise we bring.

2
Holy Spirit, prompt us
When we kneel to pray;
Nearer come, and teach us
What we ought to say.

3
Holy Spirit, shine thou
On the book we read;
Gild its holy pages
With the light we need.

4
Holy Spirit, give us
Each a lowly mind;
Make us more like Jesus,
Gentle, pure, and kind.

5
Holy Spirit, help us
Daily by thy might,
What is wrong to conquer,
And to choose the right.

W H PARKER

80 Ride on! Ride on in majesty!

1
Ride on! Ride on in majesty!
Hark, all the tribes 'Hosanna' cry;
Thy humble beast pursues his road
With palms and scattered garments strowed.

2
Ride on! Ride on in majesty!
In lowly pomp ride on to die:
O Christ, thy triumphs now begin
O'er captive death and conquered sin.

3
Ride on! Ride on in majesty!
The wingèd squadrons of the sky
Look down with sad and wondering eyes
To see the approaching sacrifice.

4
Ride on! Ride on in majesty!
Thy last and fiercest strife is nigh;
The Father, on his sapphire throne,
Expects his own anointed Son.

5
Ride on! Ride on in majesty!
In lowly pomp ride on to die;
Bow thy meek head to mortal pain,
Then take, O God, thy power, and reign.

H H MILMAN

81 The head that once was crowned with thorns

1
The head that once was crowned with thorns
Is crowned with glory now:
A royal diadem adorns
The mighty victor's brow.

2
The highest place that heaven affords
Is his, is his by right,
The King of kings and Lord of lords,
And heaven's eternal light.

3
The joy of all who dwell above,
The joy of all below,
To whom he manifests his love,
And grants his name to know.

4
To them the cross, with all its shame,
With all its grace is given;
Their name an everlasting name,
Their joy the joy of heaven.

5
They suffer with their Lord below,
They reign with him above,
Their profit and their joy to know
The mystery of his love.

6
The cross he bore is life and health,
Though shame and death to him;
His people's hope, his people's wealth,
Their everlasting theme.

T KELLY

82 There is a green hill far away

1
There is a green hill far away,
Without a city wall,
Where the dear Lord was crucified
Who died to save us all.

2
We may not know, we cannot tell,
What pains he had to bear;
But we believe it was for us
He hung and suffered there.

3
He died that we might be forgiven,
He died to make us good,
That we might go at last to heaven
Saved by his precious blood.

4
There was no other good enough
To pay the price of sin;
He only could unlock the gate
Of heaven, and let us in.

5
O dearly, dearly has he loved,
And we must love him too,
And trust in his redeeming blood,
And try his works to do.

MRS C F ALEXANDER

83 This joyful Eastertide

1
This joyful Eastertide,
Away with sin and sorrow.
My love, the crucified,
Hath sprung to life this morrow:

Chorus
Had Christ, that once was slain,
Ne'er burst his three-day prison,
Our faith had been in vain:
But now hath Christ arisen.

2
My flesh in hope shall rest,
And for a season slumber:
Till trump from east to west
Shall wake the dead in number:

Chorus

3
Death's flood hath lost his chill,
Since Jesus crossed the river:
Lover of souls, from ill
My passing soul deliver:

Chorus

GEORGE WOODWARD

84 Trotting, trotting through Jerusalem

1

Trotting, trotting through Jerusalem,
Jesus, sitting on a donkey's back,
Children waving branches, singing,
'Happy is he that comes in the name of the Lord!'

2

Many people in Jerusalem
Thought he should have come on a mighty horse
Leading all the Jews to battle —
'Happy is he that comes in the name of the Lord!'

3

Many people in Jerusalem
Were amazed to see such a quiet man
Trotting, trotting on a donkey
'Happy is he that comes in the name of the Lord!'

4

Trotting, trotting through Jerusalem,
Jesus, sitting on a donkey's back,
Let us join the children singing
'Happy is he that comes in the name of the Lord!'

ERIC REID

85 We plough the fields, and scatter

1
We plough the fields, and scatter
The good seed on the land,
But it is fed and watered
By God's almighty hand,
He sends the snow in winter,
The warmth to swell the grain,
The breezes and the sunshine,
And soft refreshing rain:

Chorus
All good gifts around us
Are sent from heaven above;
Then thank the Lord, O thank the Lord,
For all his love.

2
He only is the maker
Of all things near and far;
He paints the wayside flower,
He lights the evening star;
The winds and waves obey him,
By him the birds are fed;
Much more to us, his children,
He gives our daily bread:

Chorus

3
We thank thee, then, O Father,
For all things bright and good,
The seed-time and the harvest,
Our life, our health, our food;
Accept the gifts we offer
For all thy love imparts,
And, what thou most desirest,
Our humble, thankful hearts:

Chorus

M CLAUDIUS

86 When I survey the wondrous cross

1
When I survey the wondrous cross
On which the Prince of Glory died,
My richest gain I count but loss,
And pour contempt on all my pride.

2
Forbid it, Lord, that I should boast
Save in the death of Christ my God;
All the vain things that charm me most,
I sacrifice them to his blood.

3
See from his head, his hands, his feet,
Sorrow and love flow mingled down;
Did e'er such love and sorrow meet,
Or thorns compose so rich a crown?

4
Were the whole realm of nature mine,
That were a present far too small;
Love so amazing, so divine,
Demands my soul, my life, my all.

ISAAC WATTS

7
THE CHRISTMAS SEASON

87 Brightest and best of the sons of the morning

1
Brightest and best of the sons of the morning,
Dawn on our darkness, and lend us thine aid;
Star of the East, the horizon adorning,
Guide where our infant Redeemer is laid.

2
Cold on his cradle the dew-drops are shining;
Low lies his head with the beasts of the stall;
Angels adore him in slumber reclining,
Maker, and Monarch, and Saviour of all.

3
Say, shall we yield him, in costly devotion,
Odours of Edom, and offerings divine,
Gems of the mountain and pearls of the ocean,
Myrrh from the forest or gold from the mine?

4
Vainly we offer each ample oblation;
Vainly with gifts would his favour secure;
Richer by far is the heart's adoration;
Dearer to God are the prayers of the poor.

5
Brightest and best of the sons of the morning,
Dawn on our darkness, and lend us thine aid;
Star of the East, the horizon adorning,
Guide where our infant Redeemer is laid.

REGINALD HEBER

88 Ding dong! Merrily on high

1
Ding dong! Merrily on high,
In heav'n the bells are ringing.
Ding dong! Verily the sky
Is riv'n with angels singing.

Chorus
Gloria, Hosanna in excelsis!
Gloria, Hosanna in excelsis!

2
E'en so here below, below,
Let steeple bells be swungen.
And io, io, io,
By priest and people sungen.

Chorus

3
Pray you, dutifully prime
Your matin chime, ye ringers.
May you beautifully rime
Your evetime song, ye singers.

Chorus

G R WOODWARD

89 Every star shall sing a carol

1
Every star shall sing a carol;
Every creature, high or low,
Come and praise the King of heaven
By whatever name you know.

Chorus
God above, man below,
Holy is the name I know.

2
When the King of all creation
Had a cradle on the earth,
Holy was the human body,
Holy was the human birth.

Chorus

3
Who can tell what other cradle
High above the Milky Way
Still may rock the King of heaven
On another Christmas Day?

Chorus

4
Who can count how many crosses
Still to come or long ago
Crucify the King of heaven?
Holy is the name I know.

Chorus

5
Who can tell what other body
He will hallow for his own?
I will praise the son of Mary,
Brother of my blood and bone.

Chorus

6
Every star and every planet,
Every creature high and low,
Come and praise the King of heaven
By whatever name you know.

Chorus

SYDNEY CARTER

90 Hark! The herald angels sing

1
Hark! The herald angels sing
Glory to the new-born King;
Peace on earth and mercy mild,
God and sinners reconciled:
Joyful all ye nations rise,
Join the triumph of the skies,
With the angelic host proclaim,
Christ is born in Bethlehem:
Chorus
Hark! the herald angels sing
Glory to the new-born King.

2
Christ, by highest heaven adored,
Christ, the everlasting Lord,
Late in time behold him come
Offspring of the Virgin's womb!
Veiled in flesh the Godhead see,
Hail the incarnate Deity!
Pleased as man with man to dwell,
Jesus, our Emmanuel:
Chorus

3
Hail the heaven-born Prince of Peace!
Hail the Sun of Righteousness!
Light and life to all he brings,
Risen with healing in his wings;
Mild he lays his glory by,
Born that man no more may die,
Born to raise the sons of earth,
Born to give them second birth:
Chorus

CHARLES WESLEY

91 In the bleak mid-winter

1
In the bleak mid-winter,
Frosty wind made moan,
Earth stood hard as iron,
Water like a stone:
Snow had fallen, snow on snow,
Snow on snow,
In the bleak mid-winter,
Long ago.

2
Our God, heaven cannot hold him,
Nor earth sustain;
Heaven and earth shall flee away
When he comes to reign:
In the bleak mid-winter
A stable-place sufficed
The Lord God Almighty,
Jesus Christ.

3
Angels and archangels
May have gathered there,
Cherubin and seraphim
Throngèd the air;
But his mother only,
In her maiden bliss,
Worshipped the belovèd
With a kiss.

4
What can I give him,
Poor as I am?
If I were a shepherd,
I would bring a lamb;
If I were a wise man,
I would do my part;
Yet what can I give him —
Give my heart.

CHRISTINA GEORGINA ROSSETTI

92 Infant holy, infant lowly

1
Infant holy, infant lowly,
For his bed a cattle stall;
Oxen lowing, little knowing
Christ the babe is Lord of all.
Swift are winging angels singing,
Noels ringing, tidings bringing,
Christ the babe is Lord of all,
Christ the babe is Lord of all.

2
Flocks were sleeping, shepherds keeping
Vigil till the morning new;
Saw the glory, heard the story,
Tidings of a gospel true.
Thus rejoicing, free from sorrow,
Praises voicing, greet the morrow,
Christ the babe was born for you!
Christ the babe was born for you!

93 Mary had a baby

1
Mary had a baby,
Yes, Lord,
Mary had a baby,
Yes, my Lord,
Mary had a baby,
Yes, Lord,
The people keep a-comin'
and the train done gone.

2

Stars keep a-shinin',
Yes, Lord,
Movin' in the elements,
Yes, my Lord,
Stood above the stable,
Yes, Lord,
The people keep a comin'
and the train done gone.

3

Where did she lay him?
Yes, Lord,
Laid him in the manger,
Yes, my Lord,
Wrapp'd him in the swaddlin',
Yes, Lord,
The people keep a-comin'
and the train done gone.

4

What did she name him?
Yes, Lord,
Named him King Jesus,
Yes, my Lord,
Wonderful, Counsellor,
Yes, Lord,
The people keep a-comin'
and the train done gone.

5

Mary had a baby,
Yes, Lord,
Mary had a baby,
Yes, my Lord,
Mary had a baby,
Yes, Lord,
The people keep a-comin'
and the train done gone.

94 O come, all ye faithful

1
O come, all ye faithful,
Joyful and triumphant,
O come ye, O come ye to Bethlehem;
Come and behold him,
Born the King of angels:

Chorus
O come, let us adore him,
O come, let us adore him,
O come, let us adore him, Christ the Lord!

2
See how the shepherds,
Summoned to his cradle,
Leaving their flocks, draw nigh to gaze;
We too will thither
Bend our joyful footsteps:

Chorus

3
Sing, choirs of angels,
Sing in exultation,
Sing, all ye citizens of heaven above;
Glory to God
In the highest:

Chorus

4
Yea, Lord, we greet thee,
Born this happy morning,
Jesus, to thee be glory given;
Word of the Father,
Now in flesh appearing:

Chorus

TRANS. F OAKELEY

95 O little town of Bethlehem

1
O little town of Bethlehem,
How still we see thee lie!
Above thy deep and dreamless sleep
The silent stars go by.
Yet in thy dark streets shineth
The everlasting light;
The hopes and fears of all the years
Are met in thee to-night.

2
O morning stars, together
Proclaim the holy birth,
And praises sing to God the King,
And peace to men on earth;
For Christ is born of Mary;
And, gathered all above,
While mortals sleep, the angels keep
Their watch of wondering love.

3
How silently, how silently,
The wondrous gift is given!
So God imparts to human hearts
The blessings of his heaven.
No ear may hear his coming;
But in this world of sin,
Where meek souls will receive him still,
The dear Christ enters in.

4
O holy Child of Bethlehem,
Descend to us, we pray;
Cast out our sin, and enter in,
Be born in us to-day.
We hear the Christmas Angels
The great glad tidings tell:
O come to us, abide with us,
Our Lord Emmanuel.

PHILLIPS BROOKS

96 Once in royal David's city

1
Once in royal David's city
Stood a lowly cattle shed,
Where a mother laid her baby
In a manger for his bed:
Mary was that mother mild,
Jesus Christ her little child.

2
He came down to earth from heaven,
Who is God and Lord of all,
And his shelter was a stable,
And his cradle was a stall;
With the poor, and mean, and lowly,
Lived on earth our Saviour holy.

3
And through all his wondrous childhood
He would honour and obey,
Love and watch the lowly maiden
In whose gentle arms he lay;
Christian children all must be
Mild, obedient, good as he.

4
For he is our childhood's pattern:
Day by day like us he grew,
He was little, weak and helpless,
Tears and smiles like us he knew;
And he feeleth for our sadness,
And he shareth in our gladness.

5
And our eyes at last shall see him,
Through his own redeeming love,
For that child so dear and gentle
Is our Lord in heaven above;
And he leads his children on
To the place where he is gone.

MRS C F ALEXANDER

97 Rise up, shepherd, and follow

1
There's a star in the East on Christmas morn;
Rise up, shepherd, and follow;
It will lead to the place where the Saviour's born;
Rise up, shepherd, and follow.

Chorus
Follow, follow, rise up, shepherd, and follow;
O follow the star of Bethlehem, rise up shepherd and follow.

2
Leave your sheep, leave your sheep and leave your lambs;
Rise up, shepherd, and follow;
Leave your sheep, leave your sheep, leave your ewes and rams;
Rise up, shepherd, and follow.

Chorus

3
If you take good heed to the angel's words;
Rise up, shepherd, and follow;
You'll forget all your flock, you'll forget all your herds;
Rise up, shepherd, and follow.

Chorus

98 Sussex Carol

1
On Christmas night all Christians sing,
To hear the news the angels bring.
On Christmas night all Christians sing,
To hear the news the angels bring.
News of great joy, news of great mirth,
News of our merciful King's birth.

2
Then why should men on earth be so sad,
Since our Redeemer made us glad?
Then why should men on earth be so sad,
Since our Redeemer made us glad?
When from our sin he set us free,
All for to gain our liberty.

3
When sin departs before his grace,
Then life and health come in its place;
When sin departs before his grace,
Then life and health come in its place;
Angels and men with joy may sing,
All for to see the new-born King.

4
All out of darkness we have light,
Which made the angels sing this night;
All out of darkness we have light,
Which made the angels sing this night;
'Glory to God and peace to men,
Now and for evermore. Amen.'

99 The East Haddon Carol

Chorus
Welcome, welcome, Christ our Saviour,
This gift you bring is in our favour;
Joy and goodness to us all,
From our Saviour born in a stall.

1
Mistletoe hanging from the big front door,
Christmas presents all over the floor;
From bed we are crawling to watch the snow falling,
Pretending we're sleeping
But really we're peeping;
Excitement increasing
And joy never ceasing,
'Cause the most important person is coming to stay.

Chorus

2
Christmas cards standing on the mantelpiece,
Mother in the kitchen preparing a feast;
Cheeks are red rosy and everyone's cosy,
Outside it is snowing
And the cold wind is blowing;
Excitement increasing
And joy never ceasing,
'Cause the most important person is coming to stay.

Chorus

UPPER JUNIOR CLASS, EAST HADDON SCHOOL

100 While shepherds watched their flocks

1
While shepherds watched their flocks by night,
All seated on the ground,
The angel of the Lord came down,
And glory shone around.

2
'Fear not!' said he (for mighty dread
Had seized their troubled mind);
'Glad tidings of great joy I bring
To you and all mankind.

3
'To you, in David's town, this day
Is born, of David's line,
A Saviour, who is Christ the Lord;
And this shall be the sign:

4
'The heavenly babe you there shall find
To human view displayed,
All meanly wrapped in swaddling bands,
And in a manger laid.'

5
Thus spake the seraph; and forthwith
Appeared a shining throng
Of angels praising God, who thus
Addressed their joyful song:

6
'All glory be to God on high,
And to the earth be peace;
Good will henceforth from heaven to men
Begin and never cease!'

NAHUM TATE

Acknowledgements

The editor and publishers wish to thank the following who have kindly given permission for the use of copyright material.

John Arlott for the words of 'God whose farm is all creation'

Bell and Hyman Ltd for 'Infant holy, infant lowly' from the *Kingsway Carol Book*

Bosworth & Co Ltd for 'Thank you', words by Martin G Schneider

Celebration Services (International) Ltd, Isle of Cumbrae, Scotland, for 'The butterfly song', words and music by Brian Howard

J Curwen & Sons Ltd for 'All creatures of our God and King' by W H Draper and the tune 'Royal Oak' by M Shaw

Durham Music Ltd for 'The ink is black', words by David Arkin, music by Earl Robinson

The Executors of the late Dr Basil Harwood for the tune 'Luckington'

Herald Music Service for 'Cross over the road', words by P M Verrall

High-Fye Music Ltd for 'Stand up, clap hands', words by Alan Forrest, music by Roger Dyer; 'He made me', words and music by Alan Pinnock. © 1970 by High-Fye Music Ltd

David Higham Associated Ltd, on behalf of Eleanor Farjeon for the words of 'Morning has broken'

Leeds Music Ltd for 'Love is something' ('Magic Penny'), words by Malvina Reynolds

The Literary Executor for the late Margaret Cropper for the words of 'Jesu's hands were kind hands'

Mayhew McCrimmon Ltd for 'I saw the grass', words by Estelle White

A R Mowbray & Co Ltd for 'This joyful Eastertide' from *The Cowley Carol Book* no. 51, compiled by G R Woodward and C Wood

Oxford University Press for 'God give me ears' by J Froom from *Children's Songs of Iceland*; 'Far round the world', words by Basil Mathews, music ('Woodlands') by W Greatorex; 'God is love' by Percy Dearmer from *Enlarged Songs of Praise*; 'Heavenly Father', words by W Charter Piggott; 'He who would valiant be' ('The Pilgrim Song'), words by Percy Dearmer, music ('Monk's Gate') collected, adapted and arranged by Ralph Vaughan Williams; 'In the bleak mid-winter', music ('Cranham') by Gustav Holst, from the *English Hymnal*; 'Jesus, good above all other', words by Percy Dearmer, music ('Quim pastores laudavere') collected, adapted and arranged by Ralph Vaughan Williams; 'Life is great', words by Brian Wren, music ('Litherop') by Peter Cutts; 'Lord of all hopefulness', words by Jan Struthers, music ('England's Lane') adapted and harmonised by Geoffrey Shaw, from the *English Enlarged Songs of Praise*

David Pugh for the tune 'God of concrete'

Anthony Sheil Associates Ltd on behalf of John Oxenham for the words of 'In Christ there is no East or West'

The Society for Promoting Christian Knowledge for 'Ding dong! Merrily on high' by G R Woodward

Stainer & Bell Ltd for 'Trotting, trotting through Jerusalem', words and music by Eric Reid; 'Think of a world', words by Doreen Newport; 'One more step along the world I go', 'When I needed a neighbour', 'Lord of the Dance' and 'Every star shall sing a carol', words and music by Sydney Carter

Tro-Essex Music Ltd for 'God bless the grass', words and music by Malvina Reynolds; 'If I had a hammer', words by Lee Hayes and Pete Seeger

Josef Weinberger Ltd for 'At the name of Jesus', words by Caroline M Noel, music ('Camberwell') by Michael Brierley; 'Holy, holy, holy!' music ('Tersanctus') by Gordon Hartless; 'Lord Jesus Christ', words by Patrick Appleford; 'O Jesus, I have promised' music ('Hatherop Castle') by Geoffrey Beaumont. Copyright 1960 by Josef Weinberger Ltd

Kathryn Willis for 'Just as I am'

Every effort has been made to trace all the copyright holders, but if any have been inadvertantly overlooked the publishers will be pleased to make the necessary arrangements at the first opportunity.